DIVERSITY IN ACTION

Diversity in Politics

CATHLEEN SMALL

rosen publishing's
rosen
central®

New York

Published in 2019 by The Rosen Publishing Group, Inc.
29 East 21st Street
New York, NY 10010

Copyright © 2019 by The Rosen Publishing Group, Inc.

First Edition

Produced for Rosen by Calcium
Editors for Calcium: Sarah Eason and Jennifer Sanderson
Designer: Simon Borrough
Picture researcher: Rachel Blount

Photo credits: Cover photo of Hillary Clinton: Shutterstock/jctabb; Inside: Shutterstock: Olesia Bilkei: p. 35; Dfree: p. 12; DNF Style: p. 30; Everett Collection: pp. 1, 5, 7; Everett Historical: p. 16; K2 images: p. 32; Karelnoppe: p. 38; A Katz: pp. 17, 27; Krista Kennell: p. 39; Kolett: p. 13; Mattesimages: p. 22; Eugene Parciasepe: p. 6; Gregory Reed: p. 41; Mark Reinstein: p. 21; Crush Rush: p. 20; Gino Santa Maria: p. 23; Sirtravelalot: pp. 42–43; Spinel: p. 18; Vyacheslav Svetlichnyy: p. 25; Taras-studio: pp. 3, 29; Vyntage Visuals: p. 24; Katherine Welles: p. 8; Wikimedia Commons: Cherie Cullen: p. 40; Annie Leibovitz/Released by White House Photo Office: p. 15; Kyrsten Sinema: p. 19; Gage Skidmore: pp. 11, 36; Pete Souza, Official White House Photographer: pp. 14, 33; John Trumbull: p. 4; U.S. Congress: pp. 26, 31; U.S. House of Representatives: p. 10; United States Senate: p. 9.

Cataloging-in-Publication Data

Names: Small, Cathleen.
Title: Diversity in politics / Cathleen Small.
Description: New York : Rosen Central, 2019. | Series: Diversity in action | Includes glossary and index.
Identifiers: ISBN 9781499440706 (pbk.) | ISBN 9781499440713 (library bound)
Subjects: LCSH: Political participation—United States—Juvenile literature. | Minorities—Political activity—United States—Juvenile literature. | Cultural pluralism—Juvenile literature.
Classification: LCC JK1764.S63 2019 | DDC 323′.0420973—dc23

Manufactured in the United States of America

Contents

Diversity on the Rise

In 1788, the Constitution became the official governing document of the United States. In the original colonies, before the United States became independent from England, there had been smaller political organizations, such as assemblies and county governments. US politics as we know it now began when the Constitution was put in force and the United States was created.

At that time, there was very little diversity in politics. The United States was founded as a country of immigrants, so politicians hailed from many different countries, but aside from that, all politicians were white men who were citizens of the United States. It was not a diverse group of individuals.

The Beginning of Diversity in US Politics

This is an artist's impression of the signing of the Declaration of Independence in 1776. At that time, politics lacked almost any type of diversity.

In the more than two centuries since then, US politics has become more diverse. The United States elected its first black president when Barack Obama won the 2008 presidential election. Although there has not yet been a female president or vice president, in the 2016 election Hillary Clinton came close to becoming the first. Women now hold high positions in the government as senators and congresspeople.

In 2009, President Barack Obama broke color boundaries by becoming the United States' first black president.

In addition to women in Congress and other high political positions, there are now men and women from the lesbian, gay, bisexual, transgender, and queer/questioning (LGBTQ+) community serving, such as Tammy Baldwin, who is the first openly gay US senator.

Politics has become more socially diverse, too. In the early days of the United States, most of the white male politicians also tended to be wealthy. While family money and a background in the higher social classes can still open doors for some politicians, there are now more politicians serving who come from poor or working-class backgrounds.

Cultural diversity is also on the rise in politics. While the politicians early in US history were all either American-born or came from Europe, there are now numerous members of Congress, the presidential cabinet, state governors, and city mayors who were born outside of the United States but who have gained US citizenship.

Disabled persons are still somewhat of an underrepresented group in US politics, but that is slowly changing, too. Tammy Duckworth, an Illinois senator, lost both of her legs in Iraq, and Greg Abbott, who became governor of Texas in 2015, is paraplegic. Abbott is the first elected governor in the United States to use a wheelchair since the early to mid-1980s, when George Wallace served as governor of Alabama.

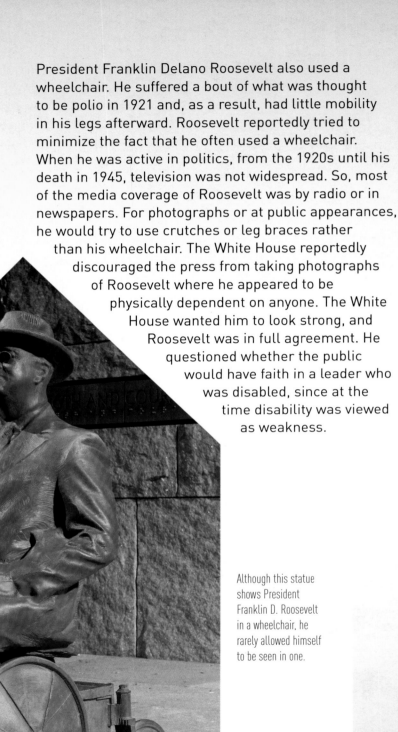

President Franklin Delano Roosevelt also used a wheelchair. He suffered a bout of what was thought to be polio in 1921 and, as a result, had little mobility in his legs afterward. Roosevelt reportedly tried to minimize the fact that he often used a wheelchair. When he was active in politics, from the 1920s until his death in 1945, television was not widespread. So, most of the media coverage of Roosevelt was by radio or in newspapers. For photographs or at public appearances, he would try to use crutches or leg braces rather than his wheelchair. The White House reportedly discouraged the press from taking photographs of Roosevelt where he appeared to be physically dependent on anyone. The White House wanted him to look strong, and Roosevelt was in full agreement. He questioned whether the public would have faith in a leader who was disabled, since at the time disability was viewed as weakness.

Although this statue shows President Franklin D. Roosevelt in a wheelchair, he rarely allowed himself to be seen in one.

The Importance of Diversity

Diversity in politics is important. It brings alternative perspectives and viewpoints to issues. People naturally see themselves and events through the lens of who they are. For example, the views of people of color are influenced by their experience growing up as members of a racial minority in the United States. Similarly, women's views are influenced by their experience as members of a gender that has been historically denied entry into certain careers and fields and/or paid less for doing the same work as men. Disabled people's views are influenced by experiencing challenges in a society that is designed for people without disabilities.

It is the same for anyone who is in some way different from the majority—in terms of gender, culture, race, ability, or economic and social background. When people from all of these diverse backgrounds work together, the result is a richer, more inclusive society. This is particularly true in politics, where the laws and policies of the United States are being formed and carried out. There would be no disability rights laws without disabled citizens and politicians working together to understand how the United States could be more inclusive of people with disabilities. There would have been no civil rights movement if community leaders and politicians had not worked together to promote racial equality. Little girls and children of color now grow up knowing that they can be political leaders because they have seen it happen. The political fabric of the United States is much richer because of the benefits diversity has brought to it.

Booker T. Washington played a key role in politics. He called for black people to progress through education and entrepreneurship.

CRITICAL THINKING QUESTION:

With today's presidents appearing daily on television and in reports on the internet, it would be nearly impossible to hide a president's physical disability. Do you think the United States would elect a visibly disabled president today? Why or why not?

Tammy Baldwin:

The First Openly Gay Senator

US Senator Tammy Baldwin was elected to represent the state of Wisconsin in 2012. Before that, she had served in the House of Representatives, representing Wisconsin's 2nd Congressional District, for fourteen years. When she officially entered the Senate in 2013, she had more experience in Congress than any of the other senators entering that year.

However, that is not all that made Tammy Baldwin stand out. After she won the Senate seat, Baldwin was interviewed by *Time* magazine, and she commented, "I didn't run to make history." But make history she did. Baldwin was not only the first female senator elected in Wisconsin's history, but she was also the first openly gay politician to be elected to the US Senate.

A Groundbreaking Election

Tammy Baldwin's election was groundbreaking. It was proof of a slow-but-steady shift toward acceptance of the LGBTQ+ community. Senators are elected by popular election. This means that each citizen's vote counts, and the candidate with the most votes wins. Democrat Baldwin won 51.4 percent of the votes cast in Wisconsin, narrowly beating out her opponent, former Wisconsin governor Tommy Thompson.

Baldwin's Beliefs

Baldwin is a progressive politician who is thought to be one of the most liberal members of Congress. In fact, during her 2012 run for Senate, her opponent cautioned voters that her far-left views could be detrimental to the country. Nevertheless, Baldwin was elected to the Senate.

SENATOR
Tammy Baldwin
Wisconsin

Tammy Baldwin made history when she became the first openly gay US senator.

SH709

As a senator, Baldwin has fought to help immigrants to the United States. In June 2013, she voted for a bill that would have enabled undocumented immigrants to gain legal residency status and citizenship. The bill passed the Senate but has not yet been acted on by the House of Representatives. Still, Baldwin remains a supporter of efforts to improve the path to citizenship for undocumented immigrants. She has clearly made her mark on US history and opened the door for other members of the LGBTQ+ community to enter politics.

FIGHT FOR EQUALITY

At the time of Baldwin's election, the LGBTQ+ community still lacked some of the rights granted to other US citizens. For example, same-sex marriage was not legal in all states. Discrimination, even though it was largely illegal, still existed.

Chapter 2

Racial Diversity in Politics

Despite the fact that the United States has had a two-term black president in Barack Obama, racial diversity in politics is still lacking. In a recent series of studies, Lee & Low Books, a publisher focusing on diversity, found that in 2013 only 10 percent of state governors were women or people of color.

Setting Records

The 115th US Congress, which convened in 2017, set a new record for its racial and ethnic diversity, according to the Pew Research Center. Nearly one in five voting members in the US Senate and House of Representatives were from racial or ethnic minorities. Nonwhite members made up 19 percent of Congress: In total, there were fifty black senators or representatives, thirty-nine Hispanic, fifteen Asian, and two Native American.

While that number is still not representative of the overall racial and ethnic makeup of the United States, it is an improvement on previous years. Just ten years before, in 2007, the 110th United States Congress had only seventy-five nonwhite voting members. In 1981, only 6 percent of voting members of Congress were nonwhite.

The biggest jump in minority groups in Congress is among Hispanic and Asian members. Both have doubled their numbers since the 107th Congress convened in 2001.

Congresswoman Grace Meng is of Taiwanese descent. She represents part of Queens, New York.

Politicians Serve Citizens

The United States is making progress toward having more racial and ethnic diversity in politics. Why is this important? First and foremost, because the United States is a diverse country in terms of race and ethnicity. White citizens make up 62 percent of the population, but the other 38 percent is composed of ethnically and racially diverse citizens from a number of backgrounds. Politicians are elected officials meant to represent the country's citizens, so in a racially diverse country, elected politicians should mirror that diversity.

A politician must serve his or her citizenship. Different groups of citizens have different views, needs, and concerns. A white politician can listen to the concerns of his or her black, Asian, and Hispanic constituents, and can try to represent those concerns in the government, but the white politician can never fully understand what it is like to be a nonwhite citizen in the United States.

Julián Castro, whose grandmother came from Mexico, was the Secretary of Housing and Urban Development under Barack Obama.

Just as a white politician cannot understand what it is like to grow up in a racial minority community, a black, politician can listen to the concerns of his or her Latinx constituents, but he or she cannot fully know what it is like to grow up with their unique racial and cultural experience in the United States. By ensuring racial diversity in politics, the government can better serve the needs of all citizens. For example, California Senator Kamala Harris is both Indian-Jamaican and a woman. So, she brings to the citizens of California her understanding of the concerns of both nonwhite citizens and women.

California Senator Kamala Harris is the first US senator of Jamaican or Indian descent.

Politicians Influence Other Politicians

Racial diversity in politics is important not only for citizens, but it also helps broaden the views of other politicians. If the United States Congress was made up of only white members, for example, those members would undoubtedly hear the concerns of their racially diverse constituents, but not as directly as they would hear those same concerns echoed by their fellow members of Congress of other races. Members of Congress hear constituents' concerns largely filtered through their staff. However, on the floor of the Senate and the House of Representatives, they hear those concerns directly from black, Asian, Latinx, and Native American senators and representatives. Hopefully, when politicians hear concerns from fellow politicians of other races, it will help them seek out different viewpoints on future issues.

CRITICAL
THINKING
QUESTION:
What do you think could be
done to encourage greater
racial diversity in US politics?

Expanding the Political Pool

Having a diverse body of politicians also ensures that there is a larger pool of qualified candidates from which to choose. If only 62 percent of the US population is white, then electing only white politicians means drawing from a pool of fewer than two-thirds of the country's citizens. If the pool is expanded to include all United States citizens, suddenly there are more than a hundred million people to choose from—and among those people, there will undoubtedly be a good number of people well qualified to be politicians.

Ensuring diversity in US politics benefits the country—the United States becomes a stronger, more open-minded nation when it embraces the backgrounds and viewpoints of representatives of all of its citizens.

Diversity in politics ensures strong representation for all citizens of the United States.

Barack Obama:

The First Black President of the United States

In the early days of the United States and as recently as the civil rights movement of the 1950s and 1960s, few people believed there would ever be a black president of the United States.

Racial tensions were so high, and discrimination was so rampant, that it seemed an unattainable dream. Even in more recent decades, black Americans have had to fight for equal rights in many areas. Black people have long been underrepresented in many institutes of higher learning and in many different career fields.

Senator First

In 2007, when the presidential race for the 2008 election was taking shape, there were only forty-seven black Americans among the 535 members of the 110th Congress. That means fewer than 9 percent of Congress was made up of black citizens. Forty-six of those were in the House of Representatives, and there

President Barack Obama, the first black president of the United States, served two terms in the White House.

was only one black senator, representing the state of Illinois. That senator was Barack Obama, and he would go on to make history by becoming the first black president of the United States.

A Difficult Presidency

Many Americans cried tears of joy when Obama was elected. People of color and white people alike celebrated an era in which the color of a politician's skin did not matter; voters thought he was the best person for the job.

Unfortunately, while Obama's election was groundbreaking and a major step toward improving racial diversity in politics, his tenure as president was not particularly easy. Racism still exists in the United States, and there were people who insisted that he was a Muslim and that he was not born in the United States. Both assertions are untrue. He is a Christian and was born in Hawaii. Although a politician's religious beliefs are irrelevant, people who bought into the stereotype that people of Muslim faith were sympathetic to terrorists also bought into the untruth that Obama was a Muslim and therefore was sympathetic, too.

Regardless of the challenges Obama faced as president, he will remain the person who truly broke the racial ceiling in politics. Not only was he the first black man to be elected to the highest office in the United States, but he was also the first minority to be—every president before him was a white man. So, for the racial minority citizens in the United States, he has opened the door to possibility.

BECOMING PRESIDENT

To be president of the United States of America, one must meet several qualifications, according to the Constitution. US Presidents must be at least thirty-five years old, they must be a natural-born citizen of the United States, and they must have resided in the United States for at least fourteen years.

Some people questioned whether Barack Obama was a natural-born citizen, but he was born in Hawaii, which indeed makes him fit that criterion.

Gender Diversity in Politics

The women's suffrage movement officially began in the United States in the 1840s, with the first women's rights convention taking place in 1848. Women in the United States did not earn the national right to vote until 1920.

Early Women in Politics

The fact that women did not have a national right to vote until 1920 does not mean that no women attempted to enter politics before then. Elizabeth Cady Stanton, famous for her role in the women's suffrage movement, became the first woman to run for Congress in 1866. She ran for a seat in the House of Representatives for the state of New York. She lost, having received only twelve votes out of the twelve thousand cast.

In 1872, stockbroker and publisher Victoria Woodhull became the first woman to run for president of the United States. She also lost. In 1887, the first female mayor was elected: Susanna Salter, mayor of Argonia, Kansas.

Elizabeth Cady Stanton was the first woman to run for the US Congress, paving the way for others like Tammy Baldwin, Grace Meng, and Hillary Clinton.

In 1916, women first broke into Congress when Montana resident Jeannette Rankin was elected to the House of Representatives. Sixteen years later, the first woman was elected to the United States Senate: Hattie Wyatt Caraway, who served for Arkansas. Rebecca Latimer Felton had served as a Senator for Georgia in 1922, but only for one day— she was appointed to fill a vacant seat for the one day between the death of a senator and the swearing in of the newly elected male senator.

Women in Politics Today

Women have not made it into the highest offices in the United States yet: No woman has served as president or vice president yet. However, in 1984 Congresswoman Geraldine Ferraro of New York became the first woman selected as a president's vice-presidential running mate by a major political party. Ferraro and her running mate, Walter Mondale, did not win the presidency and vice presidency.

Many Americans thought Hillary Clinton would be the first female president of the United States, and indeed she won the popular vote in the 2016 presidential election by more than three million votes over her opponent, Donald Trump. However, the electoral vote determines the election winner, and President Trump won the electoral vote.

Clinton campaigned hard to be the first female president of the United States, but she lost the 2016 election to Donald Trump.

CRITICAL THINKING QUESTION:
Although Hillary Clinton lost the presidency and has said she will not run again, there are a number of very powerful women in politics as of 2018. Who do you think might make a good first female president, and why?

Despite women's slow entry into US politics, women are now regularly serving in politics. There are female mayors, and women serving on state assemblies and as state senators.

LGBTQ+ Representation in Politics

Gender diversity in politics does not only include women, though. Another segment of the population is the LGBTQ+ community. Politicians who are part of this community bring an understanding of the concerns of LGBTQ+ citizens to the table and can help influence national policy as it relates to this community.

Senator Chuck Schumer of New York has been a strong supporter of LGBTQ+ rights. Here he is seen at the 2017 Gay Pride Parade in New York City.

There is a definite gap in gender diversity in politics where LGBTQ+ members are involved. As of the 115th United States Congress, there were only seven openly LGBTQ+ members out of the 535 collective members of Congress. However, it should be noted that these seven members are the only ones who openly identify as LGBTQ+. There may be others who have chosen not to disclose their gender identity or orientation.

The Importance of Gender Diversity in Politics

Men, women, and members of the LGBTQ+ community all bring different perspectives to political issues. Having a diverse body of politicians helps ensure that the interests of men, women, and LGBTQ+ members of society are represented.

Kyrsten Sinema is the congresswoman serving the Phoenix, Arizona, area. She is the first openly bisexual person to be elected to Congress.

Studies have shown that women govern differently from men. A study in the *American Journal of Political Science* showed that women sponsor and cosponsor more bills in Congress than men do, and they also bring a higher percentage of federal money to their districts. The bills that women sponsor and cosponsor tend to address education, health, and poverty and benefit women and children.

Women also tend to be more collaborative and bipartisan in politics, which was demonstrated in 2017 when the Trump Administration tried to pass a healthcare reform bill. The bill would have passed if all the members of Congress had voted along party lines—in 2017, Congress was controlled by Republicans, and the healthcare bill was backed by Republicans. However, three Republican senators flipped and voted with the Democrats: two of those who flipped were women—Senators Lisa Murkowski (Alaska) and Susan Collins (Maine).

CRITICAL THINKING QUESTION:

What do you think makes female politicians more likely to be collaborative and bipartisan? How do you think these factors might be beneficial or negative in LGBTQ+ politicians?

Hillary Clinton:

First Lady and Presidential Candidate

After the landmark presidential election in 2008 that set Barack Obama as the first black president and the first minority president, many people hoped that another barrier to diversity in politics would be broken in the 2016 election.

A Career in Politics

Hillary Rodham Clinton, former First Lady of the United States, former US senator, and former Secretary of State under President Barack Obama, was favored to win the election and become the first female president of the United States. She defeated fellow candidate Bernie Sanders to win the Democratic primary, and then went head to head with Republican candidate Donald Trump in the presidential race.

Hillary Clinton's powerful public speaking gained her many fans.

Clinton's political experience was certainly greater than Trump's. She had been a very active First Lady of the state of Arkansas and then later of the United States, and had served eight years in the United States Senate and four years as Secretary of State (the third-highest official in the executive branch of the federal government, behind only the president and vice president of the United States). Trump, on the other hand, was a business mogul and real estate developer with no political experience. Few people expected that Trump, with his lack of experience and his brash nature, would beat Clinton in the election.

In the end, Clinton won the popular vote, earning more than three million more votes than Trump. But the presidency is decided by the electoral vote, and Trump won that, earning himself the seat as 45th president of the United States.

An Issue of Gender?

Many people wondered whether Clinton's gender was the deciding factor: Was the United States simply not progressive enough to elect a woman to the highest office in the land? While that may have been true for some voters, many people had concerns about Clinton as a person and politician—with no regard to her gender. Hillary's husband Bill's presidency had been rocked by scandal, and many people felt Hillary Clinton was a willing partner in the deceit that had gone on. Further, Hillary Clinton's time as Secretary of State had been colored by accusations that she had helped cover up the truth about a 2012 terrorist attack that claimed the lives of four Americans. The 2016 election race was tainted by stories of private emails having been sent by Clinton and then deleted as part of a cover-up. Whether any of those concerns is true, we may never know, and it is impossible to say whether gender was the factor that cost Clinton the presidency. Regardless, Clinton broke a gender barrier in politics by being the first woman to run for president on the ticket of a major political party—and she was very, very close to winning.

THE ELECTORAL COLLEGE

The electoral college is used for US presidential elections. Citizens of electoral districts vote for president, and the elector for that district is supposed to cast the electoral vote that reflects the popular vote cast by the majority of citizens in that region. Although Clinton gained more votes overall, Trump's votes were spread so that he gained a majority in more electoral districts. Whichever candidate earns the most electoral votes wins. Trump won the electoral vote, but if the election had been based on popular vote, Hillary Clinton would have won the presidency.

Economic and Social Diversity in Politics

Since the United States was formed, politics has largely been a field for wealthy white men. Even as diversity in race and gender has improved in politics, a fair number of politicians still come from upper-middle-class or above backgrounds.

Money Talks

The Kennedys, who have been involved in politics for generations, are an example of such a family. President John F. Kennedy's father, Joseph, was a shrewd businessman, and the Kennedy family had strong political ties. The Kennedy sons, including John, had a wealthy upbringing, and their parents had the money and the means to help their children learn how to move among people in high society. This gained them powerful backers when they campaigned for office.

President John F. Kennedy graces the fifty-cent piece.

Money is an important factor in campaigning for a simple reason: elections are battles of ideas and personalities, and voters learn about candidates' ideas and personalities by hearing their campaign messages. Candidates spread these messages by expensive advertisements, by well-done websites, and by traveling around the country to hold rallies and meet the public. All of these things cost money. This system favors the wealthy and privileged, and when the majority of politicians are from such backgrounds, it can result in a fairly narrow view in government as a whole. Wealthy politicians see the world through the lens of someone who is accustomed to living with money, in higher-class society.

CRITICAL THINKING QUESTION:

What are some problems you think poor people in the United States face? What about the middle class? The upper class? The extremely wealthy? Are there areas in which their concerns overlap?

The problems that those with money in high-class society face are very different from the problems faced by citizens who live in poverty or have spent their lives as part of the working class.

Connecting with All Classes

Citizens become suspicious about whether politicians are looking out for their best interests when they perceive that such politicians have no idea what it is like to be poor. It is thought that this was an important factor in President Donald Trump's election campaign.

Many working-class and poor citizens saw Hillary Clinton as detached from the problems of the working class and the poor. They saw her as someone who had lived a life of privilege and wealth.

Many working-class citizens felt Trump understood their concerns and would address them.

Diversity in Politics

Some voters felt that Clinton did not understand their concerns about unemployment and poverty when blue-collar jobs were dwindling. Trump, however, focused much of his campaign on poorer areas. He promised that citizens there would see a better future if he were elected president. Although Trump is far wealthier than Clinton, voters believed that, despite his wealth, Trump could better understand their concerns.

CRITICAL THINKING QUESTION:
In what ways has President Donald Trump followed through on his promises to address the concerns of the poor? What do you think he could do to further address their concerns?

The working poor in the United States have long worked at manual-labor jobs, such as mining and construction.

The loss of jobs in the coal-mining industry has been devastating to many US workers.

The Importance of Economic Diversity in Politics

Based on 2016 estimates by the United States Census Bureau, 43.1 million Americans were living in poverty. Poor people in the United States worry about how they are going to find a job. They worry about how they are going to feed their families and keep a roof over their heads. Many are concerned about healthcare, to which they do not have easy access. They worry about how their children will break the family's cycle of poverty when they cannot afford to send them to good schools or to college. For some, they worry about how their children will avoid a life of crime, since the poverty-stricken areas of the United States are also often plagued by high criminal activity.

The middle class makes up about 50 percent of the United States population. Middle-class people also have concerns about the future. They wonder how they can afford to put their children through college. They worry about what their retirement years will look like, since many live paycheck to paycheck and do not have extra money to invest in their retirement. For those who have complex medical needs, healthcare and its skyrocketing costs are a concern.

These are issues the government needs to be aware of, and the best way to ensure that is to try to cultivate an economically diverse pool of politicians. If politicians can understand that the poor and middle class are part of the political landscape, they can ensure that their concerns are heard and, hopefully, acted upon.

Nydia Velázquez:

A Puerto Rican Congresswoman

New York Congresswoman Nydia Velázquez has brought some much-needed diversity to the House of Representatives by being its first elected Puerto Rican woman. While Puerto Rico is a United States territory and has long had a representative in Congress, it is a nonvoting member. Velázquez is the first Puerto Rican to hold a voting seat in Congress.

There are other ways in which Velázquez brings diversity to the US Congress. She is a woman, and in the 115th Congress, women make up only 19.4 percent of the 535 members. She is also from a background of poverty.

From Poor Beginnings

Velázquez was born in Puerto Rico in 1953 to a worker in the sugarcane fields and his wife. What the family lacked in money, they made up for in intelligence. Velázquez's father, Don Benito Velázquez, was the founder of a local political party and a self-taught political activist. He was interested in workers' rights and passed that passion on to his daughter.

POLITICAL FIRSTS

Velázquez has brought diversity to the political world on many fronts. She was the first Hispanic woman to serve on the New York City Council and the first Puerto Rican woman to serve in Congress. In 2007 she also became the first Hispanic woman to chair a House standing committee.

Nydia was a bright child who skipped three grades in school and in 1969 became the first member of her family to graduate from high school. She went on to the University of Puerto Rico, enrolling at the age of sixteen and studying political science. After she graduated *magna cum laude* in 1974, she began working as a teacher. Two years later, she earned a master's degree in political science from New York University and went back to Puerto Rico to teach political science at the University of Puerto Rico at Humacao.

Career in Politics

Velázquez returned to New York City in 1981. In 1983, she began working as a special assistant to Democratic Congressman Edolphus Towns. Since then she has worked in politics. In 1993, she entered the US House of Representatives after winning the 1992 election in the largely Hispanic 12th congressional district of New York.

Velázquez has not forgotten her upbringing. Her legislative policies tend toward those that support minorities and small-business owners. She is also a supporter of the National Farmers' Union, perhaps as a nod to her father's career as a worker in the sugarcane fields.

Though Velázquez returned to Puerto Rico after finishing college, she came back to New York City not long after and began her career in politics.

Velázquez is proof that anyone born to a poor minority family can successfully move through the ranks of US politics.

Cultural Diversity in Politics

Ethnic background and culture are not the same, though the two terms are sometimes used interchangeably. Ethnic background refers to the country, social, or religious group a person came from. For example, when the United States was formed, there were three distinct ethnic groups occupying the land: white settlers mostly of European descent, black slaves either brought over from Africa or born into slavery, and Native Americans whose ancestors had lived on the continent for centuries—even millennia—but who had a very different spiritual way of life from white settlers.

Culture, on the other hand, refers to the patterns of attitudes, values, beliefs, and behaviors shared by a group or population. It is a way of thinking, living, and behaving, and it includes the language, customs, beliefs, and traditions of a particular group. Although not always, sometimes culture does align with race and ethnicity. In the United States, many Asian families hold true to the cultural beliefs and practices of their Asian ancestors. Native Americans hold strong to the traditions of their tribal nation, even while living in wider society. Black families have often attitudes and values common to their experience in the United States. These are called cultural norms.

Cultural Norms

Sometimes, these cultural norms look a lot like stereotypes—and indeed, sometimes the cultural norms become stereotypes. However, there can be truth behind stereotypes. For example, there is a stereotype that Asian students are very

CRITICAL THINKING QUESTION: How many cultural groups in the United States can you think of? How many are there in your neighborhood?

driven academically, particularly in science, technology, engineering, and mathematics (STEM) subjects. While this is not true for all Asian students, it is true that, culturally, many Asian families place a strong emphasis on achievement in school. There is also a stereotype that black children—particularly boys—are very devoted to their mothers. Again, that is often true in black culture—the mother holds a significant role in the household and thus is highly regarded.

Studies on the structure of black households have noted that the rate of single mothers raising children in black families is exceptionally high compared with white families. In these households the mother is responsible for all the household tasks and also for providing the family with an income. These children, therefore, tend to grow up seeing their mother working tirelessly for the family, and they usually hold great respect for her as the family caretaker.

Muslim culture may be different from the dominant US cultures, but as more Muslims settle in the United States, their culture becomes more familiar.

The Melting Pot

These types of cultural diversity exist in the United States because it is a nation of such varied cultures. It is, as it has been described, a melting pot of cultures. Some of these cultural practices eventually blend together as families assimilate into US culture, but many of them are retained. Politically, it is important to recognize this when shaping public policy. For example, there are numerous social welfare programs in the United States aimed at helping struggling families. When these types of program are formed—and when politicians are considering whether to continue their funding—it's important for them to know who these programs serve and how. It puts a face to the issue, and it highlights the problem and why a solution is needed.

CRITICAL THINKING QUESTION:
Thinking back to the cultural groups in the United States you identified on page 28, how do you think those groups' concerns could be addressed if they had greater representation in the US political system?

The United States is a melting pot of different cultures, ethnicities, and races.

The Importance of Cultural Diversity in Politics

Ensuring cultural diversity in politics has the same benefits as ensuring other types of diversity in politics: It brings to the front a person who can identify with the concerns of a certain part of the US public and can bring those concerns to the table.

Culture influences everything people do and how they think. So, when politicians are figuring out ideas for public policy, having people from diverse cultural backgrounds weigh in on the options can bring a fresh perspective and new, creative ideas.

Congressman Markwayne Mullin is from Oklahoma. He is one of only two Native Americans who served in the 115th Congress.

According to a 2017 poll conducted by NBC and the *Wall Street Journal*, only 55 percent of Americans report being comfortable with the United States becoming more diverse in terms of culture, gender roles, and lifestyles. This is problematic given that the reality of the United States is that it is a melting pot of cultures. Cultural diversity will continue in the United States, but only roughly half of the population is comfortable with that.

Politicians can work to change this. If there is greater cultural diversity represented in politics, it will help normalize what citizens are fearing—the different cultures that, in reality, are simply different, not frightening. It is not surprising that people from other cultures want to retain their cultural identity—most people probably would not want to shed everything about who they are, simply because they entered another country. So, if the political landscape can better represent a mix of cultures, the US public can move toward more acceptance of these differences.

Sonia Sotomayor:

Hispanic Supreme Court Justice

While politics often brings to mind presidents, senators, congresspersons, and governors, there is another branch of government that also falls under the political umbrella: the Supreme Court.

Supreme Court justices are not politicians in that they do not campaign for elections and they do not lobby for particular agendas. Instead, they are nominated by the president and confirmed (or not) by the Senate. Once confirmed, they then hear cases brought before the US Supreme Court and rule on them. These cases often have something to do with constitutional law—determining whether the Constitution has been upheld by a ruling in a lower court. Often, this involves interpreting the meaning of the Constitution—should it be followed as written, or should the court take into account the fact that times have changed since it was written in the 1700s?

Politics and Court

This is where politics starts to come into play. When issues such as same-sex marriage come before the Supreme Court (which happened in 2015), the decision sometimes comes down to liberal views versus conservative views. Often (though not always), the liberal justices interpret the Constitution as a

CHANGING JUSTICE

For the first 180 years of the Supreme Court, the justices were mostly white men. Over time, this has changed. Sotomayor is the first Latinx justice.

living document, the meaning of which may change as times change. They tend to favor progressive policies on controversial topics, such as abortion and marriage rights. Conservative justices, on the other hand, tend to favor sticking to the Constitution as written, which does not leave much room for change in federal laws about these controversial topics.

Bringing Diversity to the Supreme Court

Like anyone, Supreme Court justices bring their background when they come to their job. So when Sonia Sotomayor was named the first Supreme Court justice of Hispanic descent and the first Latinx of the court, it was an important day for minority citizens. Sotomayor was born in New York. Both of her parents were born in Puerto Rico and were not wealthy. Her father had only a third-grade education, did not speak English, and was an alcoholic who died when she was only nine. Her mother worked as a telephone operator and a nurse. During Sotomayor's first three years, the family lived in a tenement in the South Bronx, and they later moved to a working-class housing project in the Bronx.

President Barack Obama nominated Sonia Sotomayor to the Supreme Court.

When she joined the Supreme Court, Sotomayor brought a fresh, unique perspective. She brought the perspective of a Latinx who grew up poor, and as a diabetic, she also brought the perspective of a person with a lifelong debilitating illness. These perspectives make her a welcome addition to the Court in terms of the diversity she brings. And certainly, these perspectives influence how she approaches the cases that come before the court.

Diverse Abilities in Politics >

The term "disability" can be problematic because, to some people, it suggests something negative: disabled people are unable to accomplish things other people can. However, the disability community does not feel its different abilities are anything to hide or be ashamed of. Today, it is no longer like it was in the days of President Franklin Delano Roosevelt, when there was a stigma attached to disability. Instead, the vast majority of the disability community proudly accepts its unique abilities and recognizes that it is a part of that group.

Disability Rights in the United States

The playing field, however, is certainly not leveled for people with disabilities. On the contrary, people with disabilities are one of the most underrepresented populations in the United States. Issues of racial and gender equality have been at the forefront of US consciousness for years, but disability rights are often ignored. For example, the landmark Individuals with Disabilities Education Act (IDEA), which ensures that people with disabilities have access to a free and appropriate public education, was signed into federal law only in 1990. Before IDEA was passed, many people with disabilities were denied access to an appropriate education, which significantly limited their long-term opportunities in the world.

However, IDEA has never been fully funded at the federal level and so its implementation is haphazard. But why is this important piece of legislation not fully funded and enacted? Simply put, disability rights are not typically a priority in politics. Politicians tend to pay the most attention to the largest, loudest groups. Racial minorities make up a large group, so legislation that impacts that group tends to get attention. Women make up a large group too, so women's rights issues gather a lot of attention. The disability community tends to be thought of as a small population, and thus it does not always attract the attention of politicians.

Not All Disabilities Look the Same

In reality, according to the 2016 Disability Statistics Annual Report published by the Institute on Disability, people with disabilities make up approximately 12.6 percent of the US population, so it is actually not such a small group. However, some disabilities are more visible than others. Physical disabilities that require people to use wheelchairs, seeing-eye dogs, hearing-assistance dogs, and other such devices and service animals are quite visible. So are certain intellectual disabilities, such as Down syndrome.

Today, children with disabilities can grow up without the negative stigma of being disabled and lead rich, meaningful lives.

However, there are other disabilities that are less obvious to the untrained eye. For example, autism is on the rise in the United States, but autistic people often pass for typically developing people—their disability often does not make them seem particularly different from anyone else. So the disabled population is not necessarily as small a group as one might think.

Cathy McMorris Rodgers, a congresswoman serving a section of eastern Washington state, has a son with Down syndrome, which is an intellectual and developmental disability.

Representing the Disability Community

When it comes to diversity in Congress specifically, the rate of disabled politicians compared to the general public is skewed. If the disability community makes up 12.6 percent of the US population, then it stands to reason that approximately 67 of the 535 members of Congress should be people with disabilities, to accurately reflect that population. In reality, there are approximately six members, or just 1 percent, of Congress who have a disability of some sort.

Although there are very few members of Congress who have a disability, that is not to say the disability community is completely ignored. There are politicians with a keen eye on disability rights. Maggie Hassan, a senator from New Hampshire, has a son with cerebral palsy, and she has been an outspoken supporter of disability rights. In 2017 Senator Hassan grilled Secretary of Education Betsy DeVos and gave her a sharp rebuke during DeVos's Senate confirmation hearings, when it became apparent that DeVos knew little about what IDEA is and how the law impacts education for people with disabilities. Cathy McMorris Rodgers, a congresswoman representing the state of Washington, has a son with Down syndrome, and she too has been a strong supporter of disability rights.

CRITICAL THINKING QUESTION:

Autistic people are known for thinking differently from people without autism. Often they are highly logical and see issues in black or white, rather than with gray areas of doubt. How do you think that sort of thinking could be helpful in politics?

In politics, it is important to have strong voices that speak for the disability community for the same reason that it is important to have racial, gender, cultural, and economic diversity: to represent the concerns of a significant segment of the population. It is not a lack of caring that makes many politicians ignore disability rights—in most cases it is an out-of-sight, out-of-mind issue. If their lives are not touched by disability, it may not even occur to them that the concerns of people with disabilities need to be considered when enacting new laws or putting programs in place.

Understanding the Unique Abilities of People with Disabilities

Often people with disabilities tend to be underestimated. For example, people with intellectual disabilities like Down syndrome were thought to be incapable of learning or contributing to society up until about the 1990s (not coincidentally, when IDEA was signed into law). Before that time, it was common to institutionalize them, where they received basic care but no real education or opportunity.

Joseph Kennedy, father of President John F. Kennedy, had a daughter, Rosemary, who had developmental and intellectual delays. In 1941, he had her lobotomized. The procedure failed and left her far more delayed than she had been previously, with the inability to walk, speak, or use the restroom. He then had her institutionalized until she died in 1961. The family rarely spoke of her, and Joseph Kennedy never visited her. She was considered an embarrassment to the family.

In the past, people with intellectual disabilities like Down syndrome were routinely institutionalized. Now, people recognize their abilities, and they can live full lives.

However, given Rosemary's IQ tests before the lobotomy, it is likely her intellectual ability was that of about a twelve-year-old. With proper education and support, she likely could have lived a decent life, perhaps holding down a job and marrying. Nowadays, people with intellectual disabilities like Rosemary's are ensured access to an education, and it has become widely apparent that they are capable of doing far more than anyone thought. They are employed alongside typically developing people, and some are even business owners. They also have a place in politics. Kayla McKeon made history in 2017 by being the first registered political lobbyist with Down syndrome.

Senator John McCain became disabled after serving in the Vietnam War.

People with physical disabilities are represented in politics, too. Senator John McCain from Arizona, for example, had physical disabilities related to the torture he suffered as a prisoner of war during the Vietnam War. He was a prime example of why diversity in abilities is important in politics. When the healthcare reform bill (a repeal of the Affordable Care Act) came up for a Senate vote in 2017, the disability community held its collective breath in fear. The bill contained provisions that would strip Medicaid of much-needed funds, and many in the disability community rely on Medicaid programs to support independent living and employment. The bill was expected to pass because, in 2017, the Senate was Republican-controlled, and it was a bill that Republicans favored. However, McCain was one of three Republican senators to flip and vote against the bill, so it did not pass. No doubt McCain, being a person with a disability himself, was keenly aware of the concerns disabled citizens had about the bill.

Tammy > Duckworth:

Bringing Diversity to the Senate

Illinois Senator Tammy Duckworth brings much-needed diversity to the Senate. Only one in five members of the Senate is female, so she brings gender diversity. She also brings racial diversity as the first Asian woman elected to Congress by the state of Illinois, and the first member of Congress born in Thailand. She is also the second Asian woman to be a United States senator, following Mazie Horono, who has served as a senator for Hawaii since 2013. In addition to being a successful female Asian politician, Duckworth brings diversity to Congress in another way, too: She is the first disabled woman in history to be elected to Congress.

Senator Tammy Duckworth is not only female and Asian, but she is also physically disabled.

Before Politics

Before beginning a career in politics, Duckworth was a military serviceperson, serving as a lieutenant colonel in the US Army. She trained as a helicopter pilot because it was one of the few combat jobs that women could perform. Duckworth was deployed to Iraq during the Iraq War, in 2004. That same year, the helicopter she was copiloting was struck by a grenade. She sustained severe injuries that cost her both legs—her right leg was amputated at the hip and her left leg was amputated below the knee. The strike also nearly cost her an arm—her right arm was broken in three places and had a substantial amount of tissue torn from it. Her injuries earned Duckworth the unfortunate honor of being the first US female double amputee in the Iraq War.

After the Army

Not surprisingly, Duckworth was discharged from military service after the devastating accident. She received a Purple Heart and returned to the United States to continue the PhD in political science she had been working on when she was deployed.

Duckworth began working for the government in 2006, and though she lost a 2006 run for Congress, she won a seat in 2012. In 2016, she announced her intent to run for Illinois' open Senate seat, which she won. Duckworth brings to the Senate a unique viewpoint on disability. Although a few other members of Congress have family members or close friends with disabilities, few members of Congress themselves have disabilities. Disability rights are an issue often overlooked in political dealings, so Duckworth's perspective as a woman with a disability brings much-needed attention to the subject.

FIGHTING TALK

Despite being a war veteran, Tammy Duckworth has been critical of the United States' war efforts. In her 2006 Democratic Party response to President George W. Bush's weekly radio address, she criticized his war strategy. That same year, Duckworth expressed her belief that the presence of coalition troops in the Middle East was making the conflict in Iraq worse. She is also in favor of stronger gun-control laws in the United States and even participated in a nearly fifteen-hour 2016 filibuster on the subject.

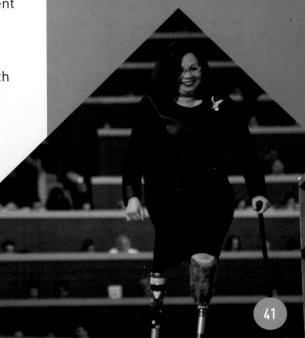

A Nation Built on Diversity

Part of the United States' richness as a nation is because of the diversity of its citizens. The nation has men and women, a significant LGBTQ+ community, people of all different races and cultures, people of different abilities, rich people, poor people, working-class people, middle-class people...the list goes on. All of these citizens bring something to the table: a world view and values that are uniquely theirs and also that are influenced by the groups they are part of.

It is well known that in any field or endeavor, diversity brings new ideas and new innovation. In fact, in the business, science, technical, and artistic fields, people with diverse backgrounds are often actively sought out for the unique ideas they bring to the table. But why not in politics? Why is politics still so heavily dominated by a single group: white men?

Perhaps this is largely tradition: when the United States was formed, the Founding Fathers were all white men. In their quest for land ownership and enterprise, as well as in the name of religion (which was a prominent force at that time), they sought to diminish Native American culture, rather than to embrace it. They took it upon themselves to try to convert Native Americans to Christianity, and they considered their views on land ownership to be the end of the discussion. Similarly, they rejected elements of black and Asian culture that came from slaves and from Asian immigrants.

Slowly but surely, the face of US politics is changing to represent the diverse people who live in the United States.

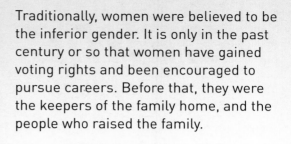

Traditionally, women were believed to be the inferior gender. It is only in the past century or so that women have gained voting rights and been encouraged to pursue careers. Before that, they were the keepers of the family home, and the people who raised the family.

In the early days of the United States, money was needed to get an education. In poor and farming families, children worked alongside their parents to contribute to the family—they were not able to attend school. It was only the wealthier families who were able to consistently educate their children—and entry into politics generally required a good education.

The United States has a tradition of being governed by wealthy white men. Tradition is hard to break and it can be a long, slow process. The United States now has women, minorities, economically disadvantaged people, disabled people, and people from many different cultural backgrounds in politics, but not yet in great numbers. As the country continues to grow and change, hopefully the benefits that a diverse pool of people bring to politics will be further recognized, and the US political landscape will begin to better reflect the great diversity of its citizens.

CRITICAL THINKING QUESTION:

What other types of diversity would you like to see in politics? Why? What benefits do you think their inclusion might bring to the US public?

Timeline

1816: John Floyd (Virginia) becomes the first Native American to be elected to the House of Representatives.

1870: With the passage of the Fifteenth Amendment to the Constitution, black men earn the right to vote.

1870: Joseph Rainey (South Carolina) becomes the first black man elected to the House of Representatives.

1870: Hiram Revels (Mississippi) becomes the first black man elected to the US Senate. He is also the first man of Native American descent to serve in the Senate.

1877: Romualdo Pacheco (California) becomes the first Hispanic man elected to the House of Representatives.

1916: Jeannette Rankin (Montana) becomes the first woman elected to the House of Representatives.

1920: The Nineteenth Amendment, federally granting women the right to vote, is ratified.

1925: Nellie Tayloe Ross (Wyoming) becomes the first female governor.

1928: Octaviano Larrazolo (New Mexico) becomes the first Hispanic man elected to the US Senate.

1932: Hattie Caraway (Arkansas) becomes the first woman elected to the US Senate.

1933: Frances Perkins becomes the first woman appointed to the presidential cabinet, under Franklin Delano Roosevelt.

1952: With the passage of the McCarran-Walter Act, all people of Asian ancestry are given the right to become citizens and thus the right to vote.

1964: The Twenty-fourth Amendment is ratified. The Amendment abolishes poll taxes (paying to vote) for federal elections.

1965: Passage of the Voting Rights Act gives all Native American citizens the federal right to vote. The Act also eliminates barriers, such as literacy tests, which were used to prevent black and poor people from voting.

1967: Thurgood Marshall becomes the first black justice on the US Supreme Court.

1968: Shirley Chisholm (New York) becomes the first black woman elected to the House of Representatives.

1981: Sandra Day O'Connor is sworn in as first female justice on the US Supreme Court.

1984: Geraldine Ferraro becomes the first female nominee for vice president by a major political party.

1989: Ileana Ros-Lehtinen (Florida) becomes the first Hispanic woman elected to the House of Representatives.

1992: Carol Moseley Braun (Illinois) becomes the first black woman elected to the Senate.

1992: California becomes the first state to have both of its elected senators be women.

2007: Nancy Pelosi (California) becomes the first female Speaker of the House.

2008: Barack Obama becomes the first black person to be elected president of the United States.

2009: Sonia Sotomayor becomes the first Hispanic justice on the US Supreme Court.

2016: Hillary Clinton becomes the first woman to win the presidential nomination from a major political party.

2016: Catherine Cortez Masto (Nevada) becomes the first Latinx in the US Senate.

Glossary

bipartisan A cooperative effort between two opposing political parties.

brash Rude, noisy, or overbearing.

cabinet A group of advisers to the president of the United States. These advisers are the heads of the executive departments of the US government.

civil rights movement A movement for social justice that took place from roughly 1954 to 1968, and involved black people working to gain equal rights to the white people of the United States.

constituents Voting members of a community.

Constitution The United States' system of laws that formally states people's rights and duties.

electoral vote Votes cast by members of the electoral college, who represent geographic groups of US citizens and decide the outcome of US presidential elections.

filibuster A political procedure where people debate over a proposed piece of legislation so as to delay or prevent a decision being made on the proposal.

Latinx A gender-inclusive form of the word "Latino," often used by Latinos who are genderqueer.

legislation A group of laws about a particular concern.

lobotomized Having undergone a surgical procedure in which a blade was used to make incisions in a part of the brain in order to treat mental illness.

paraplegic Describes a person with paralysis of the legs and lower body.

polio Short for poliomyelitis: An infectious disease that can cause muscle weakness.

popular vote Votes cast by the general voting public.

Purple Heart A distinguished military decoration for servicepersons wounded or killed in action.

stigma Disgrace associated with a particular condition, quality, circumstance, or person.

suffrage movement The struggle women fought to win the right to vote.

tenement A house that is divided into apartments that are usually overcrowded or run down.

working class People who work in blue-collar jobs.

For Further Reading

Books

Bailey, Neal. *Female Force: Women in Politics*. Vancouver, WA: Bluewater Productions, 2009.

Barrington, Richard. *Sonia Sotomayor: The Supreme Court's First Hispanic Justice*. (Making a Difference: Leaders Who Are Changing the World). New York, NY: Britannica Educational Publishing, 2014.

Denenberg, Dennis. *50 American Heroes Every Kid Should Meet*. Minneapolis, MN: Millbrook Press, 2016.

Hollar, Sherman. *Pivotal Presidents: Barack Obama*. New York, NY: Britannica Educational Publishing, 2012.

Websites

Congress for Kids
www.congressforkids.net
This site breaks down the structure and function of the US government.

Ducksters Biographies
www.ducksters.com/biography
Ducksters has links to biographies about many influential Americans.

iCivics
www.icivics.org
This fun website teaches fundamental concepts about politics through games.

Kids Discover: The Supreme Court
www.kidsdiscover.com/spotlight/supreme-court-kids/?mc_cid=1cf9ce78ac&mc eid=da9d6f62f3
This site provides a good overview of the Supreme Court and how it functions.

Index